50 Fresh and Zesty Creations Recipes

By: Kelly Johnson

Table of Contents

- Lemon Herb Grilled Chicken
- Lime Cilantro Rice
- Greek Salad with Feta and Oregano
- Lemon Garlic Shrimp Skewers
- Zesty Mango Salsa
- Cucumber Mint Yogurt Dip (Tzatziki)
- Citrus Avocado Salad
- Spicy Thai Mango Slaw
- Tomato Basil Bruschetta
- Grilled Pineapple with Chili Lime
- Lemon Poppy Seed Muffins
- Orange Glazed Carrots
- Avocado Lime Chickpea Salad
- Fresh Herb Pesto Pasta
- Grilled Lemon Rosemary Salmon
- Strawberry Arugula Salad with Balsamic
- Zesty Black Bean and Corn Salad

- Chili Lime Chicken Tacos
- Watermelon Feta Mint Salad
- Lemon Dill Potato Salad
- Pineapple Cucumber Gazpacho
- Lime and Coconut Energy Bites
- Summer Quinoa Salad with Citrus Dressing
- Jalapeño Mango Guacamole
- Lemony Roasted Asparagus
- Citrus Herb Vinaigrette
- Grilled Peach Salad with Goat Cheese
- Lemon Ricotta Pancakes
- Zucchini Noodles with Lemon Garlic Sauce
- Grapefruit and Avocado Bowl
- Cilantro Lime Slaw
- Caprese Salad with Lemon Drizzle
- Lemon Basil Hummus
- Fresh Corn and Avocado Salsa
- Roasted Cauliflower with Lemon Tahini
- Citrus Chicken Stir Fry

- Coconut Lime Shrimp Curry
- Zesty Herb Couscous
- Lemon Chia Yogurt Parfait
- Lime Honey Glazed Salmon
- Spicy Cilantro Garlic Rice
- Tropical Fruit Salad with Mint
- Lemon Thyme Roasted Chickpeas
- Avocado Cucumber Sushi Rolls
- Grapefruit and Fennel Salad
- Lemon Parmesan Kale Chips
- Fresh Garden Spring Rolls with Dipping Sauce
- Tangy Tamarind Noodle Bowl
- Lemony Lentil Soup
- Orange Basil Chicken Lettuce Wraps

Lemon Herb Grilled Chicken

Ingredients:

- 2 boneless chicken breasts
- 2 tbsp olive oil
- Juice of 1 lemon
- 1 tsp dried oregano
- 1 tsp garlic powder
- Salt and pepper

Instructions:

1. Whisk oil, lemon juice, oregano, garlic powder, salt, and pepper.
2. Marinate chicken for at least 30 minutes.
3. Grill or pan-sear on medium heat for 6–7 minutes per side until cooked through.

Lime Cilantro Rice

Ingredients:

- 1 cup jasmine or basmati rice
- 2 cups water
- Juice and zest of 1 lime
- 1/4 cup chopped fresh cilantro
- Salt to taste

Instructions:

1. Cook rice with water and a pinch of salt.
2. Once done, fluff and mix in lime juice, zest, and cilantro.

Greek Salad with Feta and Oregano

Ingredients:

- 1 cucumber, chopped
- 2 tomatoes, chopped
- 1/2 red onion, sliced
- 1/4 cup Kalamata olives
- 1/4 cup crumbled feta
- 1 tbsp olive oil
- 1 tsp red wine vinegar
- 1/2 tsp dried oregano

Instructions:

1. Combine vegetables and olives in a bowl.
2. Toss with oil, vinegar, oregano, and top with feta.

Lemon Garlic Shrimp Skewers

Ingredients:

- 1 lb large shrimp, peeled and deveined
- 2 tbsp olive oil
- Juice of 1 lemon
- 2 cloves garlic, minced
- Salt, pepper, and parsley

Instructions:

1. Marinate shrimp in oil, lemon, garlic, salt, and pepper for 15 minutes.
2. Thread onto skewers and grill 2–3 minutes per side.
3. Garnish with parsley.

Zesty Mango Salsa

Ingredients:

- 1 ripe mango, diced
- 1/4 red onion, finely chopped
- 1/2 jalapeño, minced
- Juice of 1 lime
- 2 tbsp chopped cilantro
- Salt to taste

Instructions:

1. Mix all ingredients in a bowl and let sit 10 minutes before serving.

Cucumber Mint Yogurt Dip (Tzatziki)

Ingredients:

- 1 cup plain Greek yogurt
- 1/2 cucumber, grated and drained
- 1 clove garlic, minced
- 1 tbsp chopped fresh mint
- 1 tsp lemon juice
- Salt to taste

Instructions:

1. Combine all ingredients in a bowl. Chill before serving.

Citrus Avocado Salad

Ingredients:

- 1 avocado, sliced
- 1 orange or grapefruit, segmented
- 1 tbsp olive oil
- 1 tsp honey
- Salt and pepper
- Fresh mint (optional)

Instructions:

1. Arrange avocado and citrus on a plate.
2. Drizzle with oil and honey.
3. Sprinkle with salt, pepper, and mint if desired.

Spicy Thai Mango Slaw

Ingredients:

- 1 mango, julienned
- 1 cup shredded red cabbage
- 1/2 red bell pepper, thinly sliced
- 1 tbsp lime juice
- 1 tbsp rice vinegar
- 1 tsp honey
- 1/2 tsp chili flakes or sriracha
- Chopped cilantro and peanuts for garnish

Instructions:

1. Mix mango, cabbage, and bell pepper.
2. Whisk lime juice, vinegar, honey, and chili flakes. Toss with slaw.
3. Garnish with cilantro and peanuts.

Tomato Basil Bruschetta

Ingredients:

- 1 baguette, sliced
- 2 cups cherry tomatoes, diced
- 1 clove garlic, minced
- 1/4 cup chopped fresh basil
- 1 tbsp olive oil
- Salt and pepper

Instructions:

1. Toast baguette slices in the oven at 400°F (200°C) for 5–7 minutes.
2. Mix tomatoes, garlic, basil, oil, salt, and pepper.
3. Spoon mixture onto warm bread and serve.

Grilled Pineapple with Chili Lime

Ingredients:

- 1 fresh pineapple, sliced
- Juice of 1 lime
- 1/2 tsp chili powder
- 1 tbsp honey (optional)

Instructions:

1. Combine lime juice, chili powder, and honey.
2. Brush over pineapple slices.
3. Grill for 2–3 minutes per side until caramelized.

Lemon Poppy Seed Muffins

Ingredients:

- 1 3/4 cups all-purpose flour
- 1/2 cup sugar
- 2 tsp baking powder
- 1 tbsp poppy seeds
- Zest and juice of 1 lemon
- 2 eggs
- 1/2 cup milk
- 1/2 cup melted butter

Instructions:

1. Preheat oven to 375°F (190°C).
2. Mix dry ingredients in one bowl; wet in another. Combine and stir just until mixed.
3. Pour into muffin tin and bake for 18–22 minutes.

Orange Glazed Carrots

Ingredients:

- 1 lb carrots, peeled and sliced
- 2 tbsp butter
- 1/4 cup orange juice
- 1 tbsp honey
- Salt and pepper

Instructions:

1. Steam or boil carrots until just tender.
2. In a pan, melt butter, stir in juice and honey, and simmer.
3. Add carrots, toss to coat, and cook until glazed.

Avocado Lime Chickpea Salad

Ingredients:

- 1 can chickpeas, drained
- 1 avocado, diced
- Juice of 1 lime
- 2 tbsp chopped red onion
- 1 tbsp olive oil
- Salt, pepper, and fresh cilantro

Instructions:

1. Combine all ingredients and gently mix.
2. Chill before serving.

Fresh Herb Pesto Pasta

Ingredients:

- 12 oz pasta
- 2 cups fresh basil
- 1/4 cup pine nuts or walnuts
- 1/2 cup olive oil
- 2 cloves garlic
- 1/4 cup grated Parmesan
- Salt to taste

Instructions:

1. Cook pasta; reserve 1/2 cup of pasta water.
2. Blend basil, nuts, garlic, oil, Parmesan, and salt into a smooth pesto.
3. Toss pasta with pesto and reserved water until creamy.

Grilled Lemon Rosemary Salmon

Ingredients:

- 2 salmon fillets
- Juice of 1 lemon
- 1 tbsp olive oil
- 1 tsp chopped rosemary
- Salt and pepper

Instructions:

1. Marinate salmon in lemon, oil, rosemary, salt, and pepper for 30 minutes.
2. Grill or pan-sear for 4–5 minutes per side, until cooked through.

Strawberry Arugula Salad with Balsamic

Ingredients:

- 2 cups arugula
- 1 cup sliced strawberries
- 1/4 cup crumbled goat cheese or feta
- 2 tbsp balsamic glaze or vinaigrette
- Optional: sliced almonds or walnuts

Instructions:

1. Combine arugula, strawberries, and cheese in a bowl.
2. Drizzle with balsamic and toss.
3. Top with nuts if desired.

Zesty Black Bean and Corn Salad

Ingredients:

- 1 can black beans, rinsed
- 1 cup corn (fresh or thawed frozen)
- 1/2 red bell pepper, diced
- 1/4 red onion, finely chopped
- Juice of 2 limes
- 2 tbsp olive oil
- 1/4 cup chopped cilantro
- Salt and pepper

Instructions:

1. Mix all ingredients in a large bowl.
2. Chill for 20 minutes before serving for best flavor.

Chili Lime Chicken Tacos

Ingredients:

- 1 lb chicken breast, sliced
- Juice of 2 limes
- 1 tsp chili powder
- 1/2 tsp cumin
- Salt and pepper
- Corn tortillas
- Toppings: cabbage slaw, avocado, salsa

Instructions:

1. Marinate chicken in lime juice, spices, salt, and pepper for 30 minutes.
2. Sauté or grill until cooked.
3. Serve in tortillas with toppings.

Watermelon Feta Mint Salad

Ingredients:

- 3 cups cubed watermelon
- 1/3 cup crumbled feta
- 2 tbsp chopped fresh mint
- 1 tbsp lime juice

Instructions:

1. Combine watermelon, feta, and mint.
2. Drizzle with lime juice and toss gently.

Lemon Dill Potato Salad

Ingredients:

- 1 lb baby potatoes, halved
- 1/4 cup Greek yogurt
- 1 tbsp mayonnaise
- 1 tbsp lemon juice
- 2 tbsp chopped fresh dill
- Salt and pepper

Instructions:

1. Boil potatoes until tender, drain and cool.
2. Mix yogurt, mayo, lemon, dill, salt, and pepper.
3. Toss with potatoes and chill before serving.

Pineapple Cucumber Gazpacho

Ingredients:

- 1 cup chopped cucumber
- 1 cup chopped pineapple
- 1/4 cup chopped red bell pepper
- 2 tbsp lime juice
- 1 tbsp olive oil
- Pinch of salt
- Mint or cilantro for garnish

Instructions:

1. Blend all ingredients until smooth.
2. Chill for 1 hour before serving.
3. Garnish with fresh herbs.

Lime and Coconut Energy Bites

Ingredients:

- 1 cup rolled oats
- 1/2 cup shredded coconut
- Zest and juice of 1 lime
- 1/4 cup honey or maple syrup
- 1/4 cup nut butter

Instructions:

1. Mix all ingredients until well combined.
2. Roll into small balls and chill for 30 minutes.

Summer Quinoa Salad with Citrus Dressing

Ingredients:

- 1 cup cooked quinoa
- 1/2 cup cherry tomatoes, halved
- 1/2 cup cucumber, diced
- 1/4 cup red onion, chopped
- 1/4 cup fresh herbs (parsley or cilantro)
- Juice of 1 orange + 1 lemon
- 2 tbsp olive oil
- Salt and pepper

Instructions:

1. Combine salad ingredients in a bowl.
2. Whisk citrus juice, oil, salt, and pepper. Toss and chill.

Jalapeño Mango Guacamole

Ingredients:

- 2 ripe avocados
- 1/2 mango, diced
- 1/2 jalapeño, finely chopped
- 1 tbsp lime juice
- Salt to taste

Instructions:

1. Mash avocados and stir in mango, jalapeño, lime, and salt.
2. Serve immediately with chips or as a taco topping.

Lemony Roasted Asparagus

Ingredients:

- 1 bunch asparagus, trimmed
- 1 tbsp olive oil
- Juice and zest of 1 lemon
- Salt and pepper
- Optional: grated Parmesan

Instructions:

1. Preheat oven to 400°F (200°C).
2. Toss asparagus with oil, lemon juice/zest, salt, and pepper.
3. Roast for 12–15 minutes, sprinkle with Parmesan if desired.

Citrus Herb Vinaigrette

Ingredients:

- 1/4 cup fresh orange juice
- 2 tbsp lemon juice
- 1 tsp Dijon mustard
- 1/2 tsp honey
- 1/3 cup olive oil
- 1 tbsp chopped fresh herbs (parsley, dill, or basil)
- Salt and pepper

Instructions:

1. Whisk juices, mustard, honey, and herbs.
2. Slowly whisk in olive oil until emulsified.
3. Season to taste.

Grilled Peach Salad with Goat Cheese

Ingredients:

- 2 ripe peaches, halved and pitted
- Mixed greens
- 1/4 cup crumbled goat cheese
- 1/4 cup chopped pecans or walnuts
- Balsamic glaze

Instructions:

1. Grill peach halves for 2–3 minutes per side.
2. Slice and serve over greens with goat cheese and nuts.
3. Drizzle with balsamic glaze.

Lemon Ricotta Pancakes

Ingredients:

- 1 cup ricotta cheese
- 1 cup milk
- 2 eggs
- Zest of 1 lemon
- 1 cup flour
- 1 tbsp sugar
- 1 tsp baking powder
- Pinch of salt

Instructions:

1. Whisk wet ingredients (ricotta, milk, eggs, lemon zest).
2. Add dry ingredients and mix gently.
3. Cook pancakes on a greased skillet over medium heat until golden.

Zucchini Noodles with Lemon Garlic Sauce

Ingredients:

- 2 medium zucchini, spiralized
- 2 tbsp olive oil
- 2 garlic cloves, minced
- Juice of 1 lemon
- 1/4 tsp red pepper flakes
- Salt and pepper
- Grated Parmesan (optional)

Instructions:

1. Sauté garlic in olive oil for 1 minute.
2. Add zucchini noodles, lemon juice, red pepper, salt, and pepper.
3. Cook 2–3 minutes until just tender. Top with Parmesan.

Grapefruit and Avocado Bowl

Ingredients:

- 1 grapefruit, segmented
- 1 avocado, sliced
- Mixed greens or arugula
- 1 tbsp olive oil
- 1 tsp honey
- Salt and pepper

Instructions:

1. Whisk oil, honey, salt, and pepper.
2. Arrange greens with grapefruit and avocado.
3. Drizzle with dressing and serve.

Cilantro Lime Slaw

Ingredients:

- 2 cups shredded cabbage
- 1/4 cup chopped cilantro
- Juice of 2 limes
- 1 tbsp olive oil
- Salt and pepper

Instructions:

1. Toss all ingredients in a bowl.
2. Chill for 10–15 minutes before serving.

Caprese Salad with Lemon Drizzle

Ingredients:

- 2 large tomatoes, sliced
- 8 oz fresh mozzarella, sliced
- Fresh basil leaves
- Juice of 1 lemon
- 2 tbsp olive oil
- Salt and pepper

Instructions:

1. Layer tomato, mozzarella, and basil on a plate.
2. Mix lemon juice, olive oil, salt, and pepper.
3. Drizzle over salad just before serving.

Lemon Basil Hummus

Ingredients:

- 1 can chickpeas, drained and rinsed
- 2 tbsp tahini
- Juice and zest of 1 lemon
- 1 garlic clove
- 2 tbsp fresh basil leaves
- 2–3 tbsp olive oil
- Salt to taste

Instructions:

1. Blend all ingredients in a food processor until smooth.
2. Add water as needed to reach desired consistency.
3. Serve with veggies or pita chips.

Fresh Corn and Avocado Salsa

Ingredients:

- 2 ears fresh corn (or 1 cup cooked kernels)
- 1 avocado, diced
- 1/2 cup cherry tomatoes, halved
- 1/4 red onion, chopped
- Juice of 1 lime
- Salt and pepper

Instructions:

1. Combine all ingredients in a bowl.
2. Gently toss and chill before serving.

Roasted Cauliflower with Lemon Tahini

Ingredients:

- 1 head cauliflower, cut into florets
- 2 tbsp olive oil
- Salt and pepper
- 2 tbsp tahini
- Juice of 1 lemon
- 1 garlic clove, minced
- Water to thin

Instructions:

1. Toss cauliflower with olive oil, salt, and pepper; roast at 425°F for 25–30 min.
2. Whisk tahini, lemon juice, garlic, and water for drizzle.
3. Serve roasted cauliflower with lemon tahini sauce.

Citrus Chicken Stir Fry

Ingredients:

- 1 lb chicken breast, sliced
- 1 orange, juiced
- 1 lime, juiced
- 1 tbsp soy sauce
- 1 tsp honey
- 1 tsp grated ginger
- 1 garlic clove, minced
- 2 cups stir-fry vegetables

Instructions:

1. Stir-fry chicken until browned; remove and set aside.
2. Stir-fry veggies, then add chicken back.
3. Mix juices, soy, honey, ginger, and garlic; pour in and simmer for 2–3 min.

Coconut Lime Shrimp Curry

Ingredients:

- 1 lb shrimp, peeled
- 1 can coconut milk
- Juice and zest of 1 lime
- 1 tbsp red curry paste
- 1 garlic clove, minced
- 1/2 onion, chopped
- Salt to taste

Instructions:

1. Sauté onion and garlic until fragrant.
2. Stir in curry paste and coconut milk.
3. Add shrimp, cook until pink; finish with lime juice and zest.

Zesty Herb Couscous

Ingredients:

- 1 cup couscous
- 1 cup boiling water or broth
- Zest and juice of 1 lemon
- 2 tbsp chopped parsley or mint
- 1 tbsp olive oil
- Salt and pepper

Instructions:

1. Combine couscous and boiling water in a bowl; cover and let sit 5 min.
2. Fluff with a fork, then stir in lemon, herbs, oil, and seasoning.

Lemon Chia Yogurt Parfait

Ingredients:

- 1 cup Greek yogurt
- 1 tbsp chia seeds
- Zest and juice of 1/2 lemon
- 1 tbsp honey
- Fresh berries and granola

Instructions:

1. Mix yogurt, chia seeds, lemon zest/juice, and honey.
2. Layer with berries and granola in a glass.
3. Chill 10 minutes or overnight.

Lime Honey Glazed Salmon

Ingredients:

- 2 salmon fillets
- Juice of 1 lime
- 1 tbsp honey
- 1 tbsp soy sauce
- 1 garlic clove, minced

Instructions:

1. Mix lime juice, honey, soy, and garlic.
2. Brush over salmon and bake at 400°F for 12–15 minutes.
3. Spoon extra glaze over before serving.

Spicy Cilantro Garlic Rice

Ingredients:

- 1 cup basmati rice
- 2 cups water or broth
- 2 tbsp olive oil
- 2 garlic cloves, minced
- 1–2 jalapeños, chopped
- 1/4 cup chopped cilantro
- Juice of 1 lime
- Salt and pepper

Instructions:

1. Cook rice according to package instructions.
2. Sauté garlic and jalapeños in olive oil for 2–3 minutes.
3. Stir cooked rice, cilantro, lime juice, salt, and pepper into the garlic mixture.
4. Serve warm.

Tropical Fruit Salad with Mint

Ingredients:

- 1 mango, diced
- 1/2 pineapple, diced
- 1 kiwi, peeled and sliced
- 1/2 papaya, diced
- Juice of 1 lime
- 2 tbsp chopped fresh mint

Instructions:

1. Combine all fruit in a bowl.
2. Drizzle with lime juice and sprinkle with mint.
3. Toss gently and chill before serving.

Lemon Thyme Roasted Chickpeas

Ingredients:

- 1 can chickpeas, drained and rinsed
- 2 tbsp olive oil
- Zest and juice of 1 lemon
- 1 tsp dried thyme
- Salt and pepper

Instructions:

1. Preheat oven to 400°F (200°C).
2. Toss chickpeas with olive oil, lemon zest/juice, thyme, salt, and pepper.
3. Spread on a baking sheet and roast for 25–30 minutes, stirring halfway through.

Avocado Cucumber Sushi Rolls

Ingredients:

- 1 cup sushi rice, cooked and cooled
- 4 sheets nori (seaweed)
- 1 avocado, sliced
- 1/2 cucumber, julienned
- Soy sauce, for dipping

Instructions:

1. Place nori on a bamboo mat or clean surface.
2. Spread a thin layer of sushi rice on nori, leaving a 1-inch border.
3. Arrange avocado and cucumber in the center.
4. Roll tightly, seal the edge, and slice into pieces.
5. Serve with soy sauce.

Grapefruit and Fennel Salad

Ingredients:

- 2 grapefruits, segmented
- 1 fennel bulb, thinly sliced
- 1/4 red onion, thinly sliced
- 2 tbsp olive oil
- 1 tbsp white wine vinegar
- Salt and pepper

Instructions:

1. Combine grapefruit, fennel, and onion in a bowl.
2. Whisk olive oil, vinegar, salt, and pepper.
3. Drizzle over salad and toss gently.

Lemon Parmesan Kale Chips

Ingredients:

- 4 cups kale, washed and torn into pieces
- 1 tbsp olive oil
- Zest and juice of 1 lemon
- 1/4 cup grated Parmesan
- Salt and pepper

Instructions:

1. Preheat oven to 350°F (175°C).
2. Toss kale with olive oil, lemon zest/juice, Parmesan, salt, and pepper.
3. Spread in a single layer on a baking sheet and bake for 10–12 minutes until crispy.

Fresh Garden Spring Rolls with Dipping Sauce

Ingredients:

- 8 rice paper wrappers
- 1 cup shredded lettuce
- 1/2 cup julienned carrots
- 1/2 cucumber, julienned
- 1 avocado, sliced
- 1/4 cup fresh cilantro
- 1/4 cup fresh mint leaves
- 1/4 cup cooked shrimp or tofu (optional)

For the Dipping Sauce:

- 3 tbsp soy sauce
- 1 tbsp rice vinegar
- 1 tbsp honey
- 1 tsp sesame oil
- 1/2 tsp chili flakes (optional)

Instructions:

1. Prepare the dipping sauce by whisking together all sauce ingredients.
2. Dip a rice paper wrapper into warm water for 5–10 seconds until soft.

3. Layer lettuce, carrots, cucumber, avocado, herbs, and shrimp/tofu in the center.

4. Fold in the sides and roll tightly.

5. Repeat for all rolls and serve with dipping sauce.

Tangy Tamarind Noodle Bowl

Ingredients:

- 8 oz rice noodles
- 1 tbsp olive oil
- 1/4 cup tamarind paste
- 2 tbsp soy sauce
- 1 tbsp brown sugar
- 1/2 tsp chili flakes
- 1/4 cup chopped cilantro
- 1/4 cup sliced green onions
- 1/2 cup roasted peanuts (optional)

Instructions:

1. Cook rice noodles according to package instructions, drain and set aside.
2. In a small bowl, whisk together tamarind paste, soy sauce, brown sugar, and chili flakes.
3. Heat olive oil in a pan and toss cooked noodles in the sauce for 2–3 minutes until well coated.
4. Top with cilantro, green onions, and peanuts (if using).

Lemony Lentil Soup

Ingredients:

- 1 cup dried lentils, rinsed
- 1 tbsp olive oil
- 1 onion, chopped
- 2 garlic cloves, minced
- 2 carrots, diced
- 2 celery stalks, diced
- 6 cups vegetable broth
- Juice and zest of 1 lemon
- 1 tsp cumin
- Salt and pepper

Instructions:

1. In a large pot, heat olive oil and sauté onion and garlic until fragrant.
2. Add carrots and celery, cooking for another 5 minutes.
3. Add lentils, broth, cumin, salt, and pepper. Bring to a boil, then simmer for 25–30 minutes until lentils are tender.
4. Stir in lemon juice and zest just before serving.

Orange Basil Chicken Lettuce Wraps

Ingredients:

- 1 lb ground chicken
- 1 tbsp olive oil
- 1 garlic clove, minced
- 1/2 cup orange juice
- 1 tbsp soy sauce
- 1 tsp rice vinegar
- 1 tbsp honey
- 1/4 cup fresh basil, chopped
- 1 head butter lettuce or iceberg lettuce (for wraps)
- Salt and pepper

Instructions:

1. In a pan, heat olive oil and sauté garlic until fragrant.
2. Add ground chicken and cook until browned.
3. In a small bowl, whisk together orange juice, soy sauce, vinegar, and honey. Pour over the chicken mixture, simmer for 5 minutes.
4. Stir in fresh basil, and season with salt and pepper.
5. Spoon the chicken mixture into lettuce leaves and serve.